Interviewing in Swift:

Algorithms and Data

Structures

Your guide in helping you prepare for the real world of software engineering interviews as an iOS, iPadOS, watchOS, tvOS or macOS developer. No view controllers were harmed in the making of this book.

Author: John Ngoi

Third edition, 2020

This book is dedicated to my wife, Lilian Chang, and my two boys, Jonathan and Joel in hopes that my kids pick up programming language to do amazing stuff. My wife also codes in Swift and Python. She has published iOS apps in the Apple App Store and worked on machine learning and deep learning platforms such as TensorFlow and Keras.

Jonathan started coding at the age of 8-years-old. He codes in Swift and teaches How-to-code in Swift through his YouTube channel; SwiftHamster Gaming.

Joel started his coding journey at 6-years-old, and Jonathan has become his tutor and mentor.

3

Why 3rd edition?

After publishing the 1st and 2nd edition, I received some amazing feedback from readers. I was delighted to learn that the book landed readers highly coveted software engineering jobs at some of the world's most valuable and innovative tech companies. I am encouraged and uplifted by his appreciation of how this book prepared him for the technical interviews.

New content in this 3rd edition!
After getting a lot of feedback, I am adding more content around trees. In addition, I am adding more interview questions.

All code examples in this book and in the GitHub repo have been refactored to Swift 5.2.2. The code can be considered both ABI and module stable.

If you wish to read more about ABI and module stability, head over to Apple's official blog post about this.

https://swift.org/blog/abi-stability-and-more/

Content added in the 2nd edition!
I have added some exciting new content around blockchain, including working code for a cryptocurrency written in Swift.

Why write this book?

As an iOS, iPadOS, or macOS developer, we hardly practice algorithms and custom data structures, such as stacks, queues, tries, binary search trees, and etc. That is our curse. We are actually encouraged to use the provided APIs and functions as part of the out-of-the-box framework to perform these functions. For example, we hardly write a merge sort to sort an array, we simply do .sort() and in a code review by peers, that's usually recommended and encouraged.

The world of interviewing still requires us to be able to solve these problems by applying the proper data structures, then algorithms to solve the problem without using brute force and keeping time complexity reasonable (big O notation). If you are lucky, you get to use your personal computing machine with the language and development tools of your choice. If you are not so lucky, then you will face the dreaded whiteboard.

There are a lot of guides, online materials, and books for all other languages such as C++, Java, Ruby, and Python. However, given Swift is fairly new (Swift 1.0 was released September 9, 2014), I thought I will write a book and share code on how to build these data structures, then apply them in solving problems, all in Swift. All code examples will compile and run as per the Xcode and Swift version it was written for. Below is a git repository for all the code example show cased in this book (naturally, it will change over time as I continue to add and refactor as necessary).

https://github.com/johnnst/Swift-Algorithms-And-Data-Structures

I have administered a bunch of interviews and hired dozens of developers in my 18-year-career in Silicon Valley, including being an interviewee myself. I have been both rejected and accepted by various tech companies in the valley. Take it from me, rejections always sting but take it as a great experience to prepare you for the next one.

I am only going to use this paragraph to establish some credibility. I have written numerous iOS apps that have been featured in Top Paid, Top Free, Top Grossing, and What's Hot in the Apple App Store. I also had the opportunity to reboot the Macys and Bloomingdales apps to present the first ever native iOS app that didn't suck. I helped transformed a large power and gas utility company in how the field users perform their daily tasks by delivering one kick ass app. If you are interested in stalking me online, go here.

https://www.linkedin.com/in/johnngoi

Of course, if the interview question is, "What kind of hamster will you be?", this book will not help you.

How this book is structured

We will start off by presenting common data structures that can be represented in the Swift code. Then, we will look at common algorithms and how these data structures play a part in helping to reduce time complexity.

I am assuming you know some of the basics, including Big O notation. If you really want to get a mastery on it, go buy a book on it, take a class, search the internet, or watch a video. There are tons of resources on this subject, you simply have to look.

Lastly, we will look at common interview questions and how to solve them in Swift.

In addition, there are **Practice Suggestions** and **Feed Your Curiosity** sections that help you practice and get comfortable with the concepts and how to implement these concepts in Swift.

Before you start

It is assumed that you know the Swift language or have experience writing apps using Swift.

```
let canYouReadThis = true
if canYouReadThis {
    print("Continue with this book")
}
```

If you are unable to read the code snippet above, I recommend putting down this book, and start with learning materials that is focused on learning the basics of Swift.

If you wish to learn from a 9-year-old, head here with your iPad to learn the basics of Swift.

https://www.youtube.com/playlist?list=PL4luWduXiUwcskc0qz2QCxS-RQpd22jW8

The first video of the series is titled "Learn Swift from a 9-year-old - Lesson 1: Issuing Commands".

What do you need?

As of this writing, I am writing and testing all code examples using Swift 5.2.2, so Xcode 11.4.1 is preferred. In Xcode, you can use Playgrounds to test the code and refactor as needed.

If you are using a newer version of Xcode, which usually means a higher version of Swift, you can attempt to use the Xcode migration tool or refactor it manually. With Swift achieving ABI and module stability as of Swift 5.1, the code should compile and run with the latest stable release of Xcode and the Swift toolchain.

Sending feedback

I would love to hear from you if this book does one or more of the following
…

1. Got you an awesome job as a Software Engineer or iOS developer.
    Congratulations!
2. You used this book to administer interviews, and found it useful (or
    useless) in finding qualified candidates.
3. You encountered an interview question not covered by the book.
    Send me the interview problem description, sample input and
    expected results, and the company that asked that question.
4. Have suggestion for improvements on the content of this book.
    Personally, I am always learning, and I am attracted to efficient and
    elegant answers.
5. Any future suggestions for my next edition or book!

Although I cannot promise a response to every email, I will certainly do my
best.

You can email me at code.with.ngoi@gmail.com with the **Subject Line =
"Your book sent me!"** .

Note to interviewers and hiring managers

Before we begin, this note is particular useful for hiring managers and interviewers using this book to administer one critical part of the software engineers interview process to determine if they can comfortably solve problems via code.

There is a lot of logistics that goes into getting into a smooth rhythm of hiring coders, I will not cover that in this book. Feel free to reach out to me with questions and go to the Sending Feedback chapter for how to do so.

Here's a recommended structure.

1. If possible, slot in a schedule of no more than 1 hour for the data structures and algorithms test. Buffer 10 to 15 minutes to walk through the candidate's final submission and also give the candidate an opportunity to ask questions.
2. Prepare beforehand which questions you are going to use from the "Common Interview Questions" and inform your interview panel to avoid the others from asking the same questions.
3. Each interview question comes accompanied by a difficulty rating. Here are the recommended questions for the common software engineering ranks.
    a. Principal or Staff engineer = Medium or Hard
    b. Senior engineer = Easy or Medium
    c. Below senior engineer = Easy

4. Since the Easy questions can mostly be completed within 10 to 15 minutes, you may progress to a Medium level difficulty to see if the person is able to progress.
5. What I find tremendously useful is using a timer both the candidate and the interviewer can observe. I typically ask Siri to set a timer in front of the candidate to inform the candidate that the clock is ticking.
6. Take a copy of the candidate's final work by either requesting the person to electronically send it or take a photo of the work from your smartphone.

The more successful engineering shops inform their candidates before showing up onsite where to go for study materials. A common question I get from hiring managers using my book to administer interviews is "what if the candidate is able to complete" all interview questions in this book.

My usual response to the hiring manager is "you should hire that person and be prepared to give the candidate whatever the person wants". It takes a rare individual to have the learning capacity and the coding competency to actually master every single coding challenge in this book.

Data Structures

At the core of algorithms are data structures. Knowing the available data structures and how they can be applied to solve a problem can help you avoid a brute force solution.

The data structures we will cover in this book are:

Linked List

Queue

Stacks

Dictionary (hash table)

Set

Binary Search Tree

Tric

Binary Tree

Graph

Blockchain

We will not cover out-of-the-box data structures in depth such as **arrays**, **dictionaries**, and etc since there is an expectation that you are familiar with most of them while creating apps in Swift.

Here's a recommended read on Swift collection types from Apple's documentation.

https://docs.swift.org/swift-book/LanguageGuide/CollectionTypes.html

Linked List

A **linked list** is one of the most basic data structures you will encounter. A **linked list** is a linear collection of data elements via nodes. A **linked list** can be use as the foundation to build a **stack** or **queue** data structure instead of using an **array**.

To visualize a single node, here's a popular representation (Figure 1).

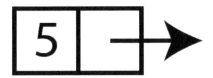

Figure 1. Representation of a single node.

Here's a linked list with multiple nodes attached to each other (Figure 2).

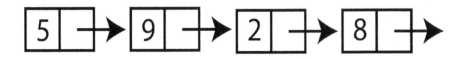

Figure 2. Representation of a linked lists.

Tip: Think of putting together a train! Your train can be as short or as long as you want it to be by adding n number of train cars. Choo choo!

Let's start coding a **linked list** in Swift!

```
/// Linked list node.
class Node {
    var value: Int
    var next: Node?

    init (value: Int, next: Node?) {
        self.value = value
        self.next = next
    }
}
```

The above is the simple construct of a node that we can use to build a **linked list**. Each node stores a value as an **Int**.

Tip: Think of all the properties you can attach to a node to make it more awesome!

```
// create the nodes
let root = Node(value: 5, next: nil)
let second = Node(value: 9, next: nil)
let third = Node(value: 2, next: nil)
let fourth = Node(value: 8, next: nil)

// then join the nodes together to form a linked list
root.next = second
second.next = third
third.next = fourth

// to test, you can see if you can print all the values from the node
// starting from the first node
var currentNode = root
```

```
print("printing a linked list ...")
while currentNode.next != nil {
    print("\(currentNode.value)")
    currentNode = currentNode.next!
}
print("\(currentNode.value)")
print("... done printing linked list")
```

The above should print ...

printing a linked list ...
5
9
2
8
... done printing linked list

A more elegant solution is to create a class for all this.

```
/// A simple linked list class.
class LinkedList {
    var root: Node?

    func insert (node: Node) {
        if root == nil {
            self.root = node
        } else {
            var currentNode = self.root!
            while currentNode.next != nil {
                currentNode = currentNode.next!
            }
            currentNode.next = node
        }
    }
}
```

```
func printNodes () -> String {
    var result = ""
    if self.root == nil {
        result = "Empty linked list"
    } else {
        var currentNode = self.root!
        result += "\(currentNode.value)"
        while currentNode.next != nil {
            currentNode = currentNode.next!
            result += " \(currentNode.value)"
        }
    }
    return result
}
}


let list = LinkedList()
let root2 = Node(value: 5, next: nil)
let second2 = Node(value: 9, next: nil)
let third2 = Node(value: 2, next: nil)
let fourth2 = Node(value: 8, next: nil)
list.insert(node: root2)
list.insert(node: second2)
list.insert(node: third2)
list.insert(node: fourth2)
list.printNodes()
```

The list.printNodes() line should return a string that contains …

5 9 2 8

Practice suggestion

Without referring to this book or any resources online, in Xcode Playgrounds, implement a **linked list** class with an insert function and a function to print the nodes linked. Test your **linked list** with the following test cases.

```
let list = LinkedList()
let root2 = Node(value: 5, next: nil)
let second2 = Node(value: 9, next: nil)
let third2 = Node(value: 2, next: nil)
let fourth2 = Node(value: 8, next: nil)
list.insert(root2)
list.insert(second2)
list.insert(third2)
list.insert(fourth2)
// print your nodes in order of insertion
```

Queue

If you just came from the **linked list** chapter, it is possible to build a **queue** using a **linked list**. However, unless explicitly asked to do so, you can simply use the out-of-the-box **array** data structure. This will save you a lot of time during the interview and is far easier to implement.

The main difference between a **queue** and a **stack** is these two acronyms; **FIFO** and **LIFO** respectively.

FIFO = First In First Out (queue)
LIFO = Last In First Out (stack)

We will cover **stacks** in the next chapter.

To implement a **queue** mechanism fairly quickly, here are some code to do so using an **array**.

```
// create your array with values
var q = [2, 5, 7, 8, 9, 12, 6]

// enqueue
q.append(4)
print(q) // prints [2, 5, 7, 8, 9, 12, 6, 4]

// dequeue
let value = q.removeFirst()
print(q) // prints [5, 7, 8, 9, 12, 6, 4]
```

Easy right?! The takeaway concept here is the **enqueue** and **dequeue** which are core functions of a **queue**.

A more challenging question is "when" to use them?

Here's how you would implement a **queue** class.

```
// queue class
class Queue {
    var qu = [Int]()

    func enqueue (value: Int) {
        qu.append(value)
    }

    func dequeue () -> Int? {
        if qu.count > 0 {
            return qu.removeFirst()
        }
        return nil
    }
}

let q2 = Queue()
q2.enqueue(5)
q2.enqueue(9)
q2.enqueue(3)
print(q2.qu) // prints [5, 9, 3]
let v2 = q2.dequeue()
print(q2.qu) // prints [9, 3]
```

The **queue** data structure is particularly useful in **Breadth First Search** and **Dijkstra's** algorithm. Think of using **queues** to keep track of your progress or scan through a **graph** or **tree**. We will cover these algorithms in a later chapter.

Practice suggestion

Without referring to this book or any resources online, in Xcode Playgrounds, implement a **queue** class with **enqueue** and **dequeue** functions. Test your **queue** with the following test cases.

```
let q2 = Queue()
q2.enqueue(5)
q2.enqueue(9)
q2.enqueue(3)
print(q2.qu) // prints [5, 9, 3]
let v2 = q2.dequeue()
print(q2.qu) // prints [9, 3]
```

Advice: It is alright to peek at the book the first few times! The secret here is practice. Keep practicing until you can get this done, and take a break from each attempt.

Feed your curiosity

Hopefully by now, you know how to implement a **linked list** and **queue** without any help of this book. Either way, if you want to feed your curiosity some more, try implementing a **queue** using a **linked list** instead of using an array.

If you just want to read up on it, an example is available in Appendix A.

Stack

In the previous chapter, we covered the **queue** data structure. **Stacks** are similar except you **push** and **pop**.

To implement simple **stack** functions using an **array**, here is some code for it.

```
// create your array with values
var s = [2, 5, 7, 3]

// push
s.append(9)
print(s) // print [2, 5, 7, 3, 9]

// pop
let pop = s.removeLast() // the variable pop now has a value of 9
print(s) // print [2, 5, 7, 3]
```

To implement a **stack** class, here's the code for it.

```
// stack class
class Stack {
    var stack = [Int]()

    func push (value: Int) {
        stack.append(value)
    }

    func pop () -> Int? {
        if stack.count > 0 {
            return stack.removeLast()
```

```
        }
        return nil
    }
}

let stack = Stack()
stack.push(2)
stack.push(5)
stack.push(7)
stack.push(3)
print(stack.stack) // prints [2, 5, 7, 3]
let value = stack.pop()
print(stack.stack) // prints [2, 5, 7]
```

The **stack** data structure is particularly useful in **Depth First Search** algorithms. Also think of a way to keep track of progress and used in reversing order or backtracking. We will cover algorithms using **stacks** in a later chapter.

Practice suggestion

Without referring to this book or any resources online, in Xcode Playgrounds, implement a **stack** class with push and pop functions. Test your **queue** with the following test cases.

```
let stack = Stack()
stack.push(2)
stack.push(5)
stack.push(7)
stack.push(3)
print(stack.stack) // prints [2, 5, 7, 3]
let value = stack.pop()
print(stack.stack) // prints [2, 5, 7]
```

Feed your curiosity

Hopefully by now, you know how to implement a **linked list** and **stack** without any help of this book. Either way, if you want to feed your curiosity some more, try implementing a **stack** using a linked list instead of using an **array**.

If you just want to read up on it, an example is available in Appendix A.

Dictionary

Dictionaries are very powerful data structures to allow for quick access of values through keys. They are a type of hash table and sometimes referred to as a hash map as well. If you see an algorithm from another language using hash tables or hash maps, in most cases, you can easily us a Dictionary in your Swift algorithms.

Time complexity good to know.

Insertion = often O(1)
Deletion = often O(1)
Retrieval = often O(1)

Apple provides documentation on **Dictionaries** here.

https://developer.apple.com/library/ios/documentation/Swift/Conceptual/Swift_Programming_Language/CollectionTypes.html

We are not going to cover time complexity in detail and I do highly recommend you read up on it by searching the internet. If you are currently in a Computer Science type course, this topic is usually covered early on. It is very important to at least have a fundamental understanding of how to measure time complexity of a given code if you plan to go far as a software engineer.

Set

Sets are very useful data structures that helps guarantee uniqueness.

Time complexity good to know.

Insertion = often $O(n)$, because it is checking every single item for equality
Deletion = often $O(1)$
Retrieval = often $O(1)$

In algorithms, **sets** are amazing in ensuring uniqueness, and also improve your overall time complexity if you need a fast way to check if an item is computed or visited if the order of the items does not matter due to the $O(1)$ retrieval time.

Apple covers documentation on **Sets** here.

https://developer.apple.com/library/ios/documentation/Swift/Conceptual/Swift_Programming_Language/CollectionTypes.html

Breathe ...

You are about to embark on more advance data structures.

If you want to take a break, take a walk, get some perspective, watch a dumb show to balance all this knowledge you are gaining, this is a good point in the book to do so.

If you need recommendations on my favorite dumb movies, email me at code.with.ngoi@gmail.com with the subject line "Recommend me a dumb movie!"

If you are enjoying the book so far, don't forget to leave a rating and review! Go to the link below to review the book!!

https://www.amazon.com/Interviewing-Swift-Algorithms-Structures-engineering-ebook-dp-B01L8DY5H6/dp/B01L8DY5H6/ref=mt_kindle?_encoding=UTF8&me=&qid=

Binary Search Tree (BST)

Next up, the tree structures. We will cover **binary search trees (BST)** and **tries**, two data structures that are common in solving interview problems.

Here's what a **BST** looks like if you need to visualize (Figure 3).

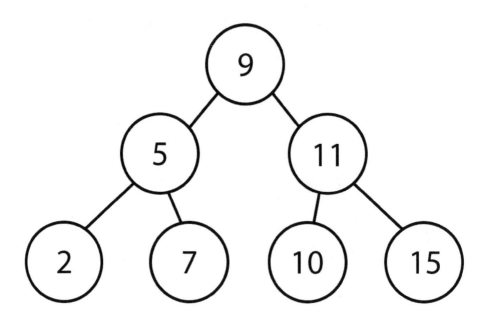

Figure 3. Representation of a BST.

Why use a **BST** or even learn this concept?

A couple of simple reasons:

1. As you implement a **BST**, notice things are sorted. We should like things when they are sorted as you can make certain assumptions. *Hint: Go left or go right!*
2. Also notice that you should attempt to rebalance the tree as you continue to insert or delete nodes in the tree.
3. Another thing to observe is that the time complexity to find something in a tree is usually less than O(n) because of #1 and #2.
4. Recursion technics are popular when dealing with a tree and recommended to achieve the ideal time complexity.
5. Finally, **BST** type questions do come up quite often in interviews.

Below is a simple implementation of **BST** in Swift.

Approach:

1. First, learn how a basic tree node is constructed and initialized. Similar to how a linked list node is constructed, understand the similarities and differences. Learn to love creating nodes of all types!
2. Next, learn how to implement node insertion into **BST**.

3. Off course, you need a method in order to test if your **BST** is implemented correctly by printing the node values in order. This will teach you one way to traverse a **BST** via recursion.

```
/// Simple tree node class.
class TreeNode {
    var data: Int = 0
    var left: TreeNode?
    var right: TreeNode?

    init(data: Int) {
        self.data = data
    }
}

// Implement an insert function to create the BST.

/// Insert a node into a tree.
///
/// - Parameters:
///     - root: Tree root node.
///     - node: Node to be inserted.
func insert (root: TreeNode?, node: TreeNode) {
    // for more advance Swift programmers, you can start of with "if
let else" pattern
    // this is more readable for general audience coming from other
languages
    if root == nil {
        return
    } else {
        if let root = root {
            if root.data > node.data { // go left
                if root.left == nil {
                    root.left = node
```

```swift
            } else {
                insert(root: root.left, node: node)
            }
        } else { // go right
            if root.right == nil {
                root.right = node
            } else {
                insert(root: root.right, node: node)
            }
        }
    }
}

// Test the implementation of the BST.

/// Print the tree nodes in ascending order.
///
/// - Parameter root: Tree root node.
func printTreeInOrder (root: TreeNode?) {
    if root == nil {
        return
    }
    if let root = root {
        printTreeInOrder(root: root.left)
        print(root.data)
        printTreeInOrder(root: root.right)
    }
}

let root = TreeNode(data: 9)
insert(root: root, node: TreeNode(data: 7))
insert(root: root, node: TreeNode(data: 11))
insert(root: root, node: TreeNode(data: 5))
insert(root: root, node: TreeNode(data: 15))
insert(root: root, node: TreeNode(data: 21))
```

```
insert(root: root, node: TreeNode(data: 6))
printTreeInOrder(root: root)
```

printTreeInOrder(root) should print …

```
5
6
7
9
11
15
21
```

Congratulations! You now know how to implement a **BST**.

One main consideration to take away before declaring complete victory, is that this method takes no attempt at rebalancing the **BST** for optimized queries. You can most certainly go deep on **BST** beyond this book and maybe come up with a new type of **BST** that is far more efficient in time complexity and space complexity!

Here are some fundamental BST operations to look at beyond this book.

Insertion
Searching
Deletion

Also look at how to balance a tree, and understand concepts such as self-balancing BST.

Again, you can search the internet for knowledge or go take a class! Or better yet, motivate me to write a book about it!

Practice suggestion

Without referring to this book or any resources online, in Xcode Playgrounds, implement a **BST** class with an insert function to create your tree. Then to test, create a function to print out all the nodes in order. Test your **BST** with the following test cases.

```
let root = TreeNode(data: 9)
insert(root, node: TreeNode(data: 7))
insert(root, node: TreeNode(data: 11))
insert(root, node: TreeNode(data: 5))
insert(root, node: TreeNode(data: 15))
insert(root, node: TreeNode(data: 21))
insert(root, node: TreeNode(data: 6))
// this line is for your print function
```

Trie

The next tree to look at, and my personal favorite tree data structure is a **trie**. The reason why this is my personal favorite is that it helps solve a very relevant human problem, and the way it is constructed is pretty clever. A **trie** is very useful for solving word problems with efficient time complexity.

The magic sauce to a **trie** is the use of a **map** (Swift **Dictionary**).

Below is a simple **trie**.

Approach:

1. First, learn how to construct and initialize a **trie** node. This is very important!
2. Next, learn how to implement insertion of a **trie** node in an efficient time complexity.
3. Lastly, learn how to test your code by implementing a find word function.

```
/// Simple trie node class.
class TrieNode {
    var char: Character = "\0" // that's a null character
    var isWord = false // very important to flag a node as a word
    private var children = [Character: TrieNode]() // the magic
sauce, set to private to avoid accidents

    init (char: Character, isWord: Bool) {
```

```swift
            self.char = char
            self.isWord = isWord
        }


        func getChildren() -> [Character: TrieNode] {
            return children
        }


        func getChild(for char: Character) -> TrieNode? {
            if let child = self.children[char] {
                return child
            }
            return nil
        }


        func addChild(for char: Character, isWord: Bool) {
            if children[char] == nil {
                children[char] = TrieNode(char: char, isWord: isWord)
            }
        }


        func update(isWord: Bool) {
            self.isWord = isWord
        }

    }


    /// A simple trie class.
    class Trie {
        var root = TrieNode(char: "\0", isWord: false)

        /// Inserts the word into the trie.
        ///
        /// - Parameter word: Text to be inserted.
        func insert (word: String) {
```

```
        if word.count > 0 { // protect your trie, don't allow zero
characters
            var currentNode: TrieNode = self.root
            for (index, char) in word.enumerated() {
                let isWord = word.count == (index + 1) ? true : false
                if let childNode = currentNode.getChild(for: char) {
                    if isWord {
                        childNode.update(isWord: true)
                        break
                    }
                } else {
                    currentNode.addChild(for: char, isWord: isWord)
                }
                currentNode = currentNode.getChild(for: char)!
            }
        }
    }


    /// Look up a word from the trie.
    ///
    /// - Parameter word: Text to look up.
    /// - Returns: (true) if found; (false) if not.
    func find (word: String) -> Bool {
        if word.count > 0 {
            var currentNode: TrieNode = self.root
            for (index, char) in word.enumerated() {
                print("""

                    find word stats
                    index = \(index)
                    char = \(char)
                    currentNode.char = \(currentNode.char)
                    currentNode.isWord = \(currentNode.isWord)
                    """)
                if let childNode = currentNode.getChild(for: char) {
                    print("""
```

```
                            childNode.char = \(childNode.char)
                            childNode.isWord = \(childNode.isWord)
                            """)
                    if index == (word.count - 1) {
                        if childNode.isWord == true {
                            print("found word \(word)")
                            return true
                        }
                    }
                } else {
                    print("did not find \(word)")
                    return false
                }
                if let childNode = currentNode.getChild(for: char) {
                    currentNode = childNode
                }
            }
        }
        print("did not find \(word)")
        return false
    }
}

// let's test the trie

let trie = Trie()
trie.insert(word: "john")
trie.find(word: "john") // returns true
trie.find(word: "jon") // returns false
trie.find(word: "lilian") // returns false
trie.insert(word: "lilian")
trie.find(word: "lilian") // returns true
trie.find(word: "lillian") // returns false
trie.insert(word: "jonathan")
trie.insert(word: "joel")
trie.find(word: "john") // returns true
```

```
trie.find(word: "jon") // returns false
trie.find(word: "jonathen") // returns false
trie.find(word: "joel") // returns true
trie.find(word: "jonathan") // returns true
trie.find(word: "james") // returns false
trie.insert(word: "jim")
trie.insert(word: "james")
trie.find(word: "jimbo") // returns false
trie.find(word: "james") // returns true
```

Now that you know how **tries** are implemented, it is quite fascinating to see it in action.

Practice suggestion

Without referring to this book or any resources online, in Xcode Playgrounds, implement a **trie** class with insert and find word functions. Test your **trie** with the following test cases.

```
let trie = Trie()
trie.insert("john")
trie.find("john") // returns true
trie.find("jon") // returns false
trie.find("lilian") // returns false
trie.insert("lilian")
trie.find("lilian") // returns true
```

Binary Tree (BT)

Here is an example Binary Tree.

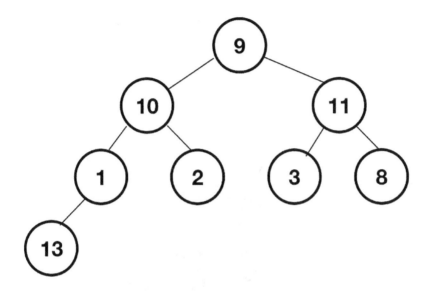

Figure 4. Representation of a Binary Tree

From the previous chapters on **Binary Search Tree (BST)** and **Trie**, why the heck do we need a binary tree?

Let's first start with the comparison between a binary search tree and a binary tree.

Binary Tree	Binary Search Tree
Binary Tree is a non-linear data structure made out of nodes.	A BST is an "ordered binary tree" where the left node value is less than the current node value, and the right node value is greater than the current node value.
Insertion, deletion, and searching is slower than BST due to its unordered nature.	Insertion, deletion, searching is faster than Binary Tree due to the ordered characteristics.
Searching a binary tree takes O(n).	Searching a BST takes O(h), where h is the height of the tree. Searching a balanced BST takes O(log n). It is possible for a BST to degenerate into a linked list, which then takes O(n), which is the big O for a Linked List.

Just like a BST, a binary tree node basic construction is pretty much the same.

```
class Node {
    var value: Int
    var left: Node?
    var right: Node?

    init(value: Int) {
        self.value = value
    }
}
```

This is where the difference begins. When you are asked to insert nodes into a binary tree, typically, the preferred way to insert new nodes is through level order to keep the BT balanced. A balanced BT means that for any two leaf nodes, the difference in depth is at most 1.

We will cover the ways to traverse a tree in a later chapter; inorder, preorder, postorder, and level order.

Below is an example of how to implement a BT.

```
class Node {
    var value: Int
    var left: Node?
    var right: Node?

    init(value: Int) {
        self.value = value
    }

    class func insert(value: Int, root: Node) {
        var queue = [Node]()
        queue.append(root)

        while !queue.isEmpty {
            let node = queue.removeFirst() // dequeue
            if let left = node.left {
                queue.append(left)
            } else {
                node.left = Node(value: value)
                break
            }

            if let right = node.right {
                queue.append(right)
            } else {
                node.right = Node(value: value)
                break
            }
        }
    }

    class func printInOrder(root: Node) {
        if let left = root.left {
```

```
            printInOrder(root: left)
        }
        print(root.value)
        if let right = root.right {
            printInOrder(root: right)
        }
    }
}


// Let's test!
let root1 = Node(value: 9)
Node.insert(value: 10, root: root1)
Node.insert(value: 11, root: root1)
Node.insert(value: 1, root: root1)
Node.insert(value: 2, root: root1)
Node.insert(value: 3, root: root1)
Node.insert(value: 8, root: root1)
Node.insert(value: 13, root: root1)
Node.printInOrder(root: root1)
```

The above test will print in this order.

```
13
1
10
2
9
3
11
8
```

Tree Traversals (Inorder, Preorder, Postorder, Level Order)

There are 4 common ways to traverse a tree in a particular order, they are inorder, preorder, postorder, and level order.

These are very important concepts to get a strong grasp of, as a lot of tree type algorithms will expect you to use one of these traversals to solve a problem in acceptable time and space complexity.

This sounds confusing!? What's the trick to learning them?

First, you must get comfortable constructing a Binary Tree or a Binary Search Tree. Revisit the previous chapters on them before continuing here.

The first three, are considered Depth First traversals. The level order is considered a Breadth First traversal. We will also cover Depth First Search (DFS) and Breadth First Search (BFS) algorithms using similar strategies in later chapters. DFS and BFS algorithms are very important to have in your toolkit!

Think about how a tree is constructed regardless if it is a BST or BT. The tree is created from nodes, and each node has a left or right child node, or both. There is always a root node (the node that starts the tree) and all these algorithms starts at the root node.

For a visual, here is an example BT.

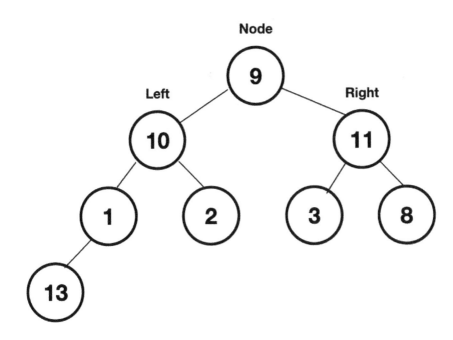

Figure 5. Example Binary Tree

Here's a simple summary of each traversals. We will also use the example BT illustrated to showcase the output for each traversal.

Learning Tip: Based on the output of each traversal, use a pencil or your finger to trace how the BT is traversed from the BT illustration in the figure above.

Depth First Traversals

Inorder: Left, Root, Right: 13, 1, 10, 2, 9, 3, 11, 8

Preorder: Root, Left, Right: 9, 10, 1, 13, 2, 11, 3, 8

Postorder: Left, Right, Root: 13, 1, 2, 10, 3, 8, 11, 9

Breadth First Traversal

Level Order: (scans the tree horizontally using a queue): 9, 10, 11, 1, 2, 3, 8, 13

Since all 4 traversals visits every node, the time complexity for each algorithm is O(n). To compare, for a balanced BST, the insertion and searching can be perform much faster since it takes O(log n) time.

For inorder, preorder, and postorder (Depth First traversals), the space complexity is O(h), where h is the height of the tree. Since it uses recursion to traverse either the right or left nodes, you can visualize the call stack only needing h space instead of n. We can also consider that $h <= n$.

For level order traversal, it uses O(n) space because it uses a queue to perform a Breadth First traversal.

One immediate benefit of these traversals is to help print and validate that the tree constructed is correct, and it is something you can also use in your unit tests.

Below are examples of the traversal algorithms.

For reference, here is the implementation of a tree node.

```swift
class Node {
    var value: Int
    var left: Node?
    var right: Node?

    init(_ value: Int) {
        self.value = value
    }
}
```

Inorder (Left, Root, Right):

```swift
func printInorder(_ node: Node?) {
    guard let node = node else { return }

    printInorder(node.left)  // Left
    print(node.value)        // Root
    printInorder(node.right) // Right
}
```

Preorder (Root, Left, Right):

```swift
func printPreorder(_ node: Node?) {
    guard let node = node else { return }

    print(node.value)         // Root
    printPreorder(node.left)  // Left
    printPreorder(node.right) // Right
}
```

Postorder (Left, Right, Root):

```swift
func printPostorder(_ node: Node?) {
    guard let node = node else { return }

    printPostorder(node.left)  // Left
    printPostorder(node.right) // Right
    print(node.value)          // Root
}
```

Level Order (uses a queue to traverse the tree horizontally, BFS):

```swift
func printLevelOrder() {
    var queue = [Node]()
    queue.append(root)

    while !queue.isEmpty {
        let node = queue.removeFirst()
        print(node.value)
        if let left = node.left {
            queue.append(left)
        }

        if let right = node.right {
            queue.append(right)
        }
    }
}
```

Check out the full working example on GitHub, and look for the *TreeTraversals.playground.*

Graph

Next up, the dreaded **graph**.

Three main concept you need to grasp.

1. **Vertex**. Like a **linked list** or **BST**, vertices are basically nodes. You need to master creating simple **graph** nodes to advance further. To make it more relevant in your interview, we will use the term **vertex** instead of node for this chapter.

2. **Edge**. An **edge** connects two **vertices**. It can be one way (directed) or two way (undirected).

3. **Weight**. To make **edges** more relevant in real world problems, **edges** can show the cost to go from one **vertex** to another **vertex** as **weights**.

Based on the 3 concepts above, below is a simple **graph** implementation in Swift.

```
/// Simple vertex class.
class Vertex {
    var key: String?
    var neighbors: [Edge]

    init () {
        self.neighbors = [Edge]()
    }

    init (key: String) {
```

```swift
        self.key = key
        self.neighbors = [Edge]()
    }
}


/// Simple edge class.
class Edge {
    var neighbor: Vertex
    var weight: Int

    init () {
        self.weight = 0
        self.neighbor = Vertex()
    }
}


/// Simple graph class.
class Graph {
    var canvas: [Vertex]
    var isDirected: Bool

    init() {
        self.canvas - [Vertex]()
        self.isDirected = true
    }

    func addVertex (key: String) -> Vertex {
        // create a vertex with the key
        let childVertex: Vertex = Vertex(key: key)

        // add vertex to graph canvas
        canvas.append(childVertex)
        return childVertex
    }

    func addEdge (source: Vertex, neighbor: Vertex, weight: Int) {
```

```
        // create a new edge
        let newEdge = Edge()
        newEdge.neighbor = neighbor
        newEdge.weight = weight
        source.neighbors.append(newEdge)

        // check for undirected graph
        if isDirected == false {
            // create a reverse edge
            let reverseEdge = Edge()
            reverseEdge.neighbor = source
            reverseEdge.weight = weight
            neighbor.neighbors.append(reverseEdge)
        }
    }
}


// test your graph code
let graph = Graph()
let vertex1 = graph.addVertex(key: "G")
let vertex2 = graph.addVertex(key: "H")
let vertex3 = graph.addVertex(key: "A")
let vertex4 = graph.addVertex(key: "C")
let vertex5 = graph.addVertex(key: "Z")
graph.addEdge(source: vertex1, neighbor: vertex2, weight: 5)
graph.addEdge(source: vertex1, neighbor: vertex3, weight: 1)
graph.addEdge(source: vertex1, neighbor: vertex5, weight: 11)
graph.addEdge(source: vertex2, neighbor: vertex4, weight: 1)
graph.addEdge(source: vertex4, neighbor: vertex5, weight: 2)
```

Challenge!

Can you draw what the **graph** looks like from the example above? Answer is revealed in Appendix A.

How do I really test this?

Nice work, you now know how to implement a **graph** in Swift. Printing the **array** within the **graph** object will just show the **vertex** values as it was inserted. That's kinda pointless. At most, it just validates the objects were added to the **graph array**, but not validate that the **graph** was properly created.

A meaningful test for a **graph** would be to find a **vertex** in a **graph**, or find the shortest path between two **vertices**.

We can employ **Breadth First Search** to find a vertex, and **Dijkstra's algorithm** to find shortest path. We will cover this in a later chapter.

Practice suggestion

Without referring to this book or any resources online, in Xcode Playgrounds, implement a **graph** class that will add vertices and edges to create a graph. Use the test below.

```
// test your graph code
let graph = Graph()
let vertex1 = graph.addVertex("G")
let vertex2 = graph.addVertex("H")
let vertex3 = graph.addVertex("A")
let vertex4 = graph.addVertex("C")
let vertex5 = graph.addVertex("Z")
graph.addEdge(vertex1, neighbor: vertex2, weight: 5)
graph.addEdge(vertex1, neighbor: vertex3, weight: 1)
graph.addEdge(vertex1, neighbor: vertex5, weight: 11)
graph.addEdge(vertex2, neighbor: vertex4, weight: 1)
graph.addEdge(vertex4, neighbor: vertex5, weight: 2)
```

Blockchain

Heard of Bitcoin?

Cryptocurrency mania swept the world, and we saw crazy fluctuation of all sorts of cryptocurrencies from Bitcoin, Litecoin, Ethereum and too many to name here. Some startups, looking to raise funds, resorted to Initial Coin Offering (ICO).

At peak, Bitcoin was valued at USD 19,783.06. If you bought a pizza with 10 Bitcoin before the peak, that pizza would have cost you USD 197,830.60 at peak.

That's one expensive pizza!

Cryptocurrency is here to stay, it has forever changed how humans view and use currency. The technology behind cryptocurrency is called blockchain.

In this chapter, we will discuss what blockchain is, the fundamentals you need to know, and how to implement a simple blockchain algorithm to create your own cryptocurrency in Swift, including a sample mining test to showcase how it all works.

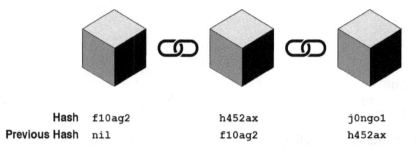

Hash	f10ag2	h452ax	j0ngo1
Previous Hash	nil	f10ag2	h452ax

Figure 4. Blockchain illustration.

The fundamentals of blockchain:

1. A blockchain is made up of blocks. If you remember the Linked List chapter, it has some similarities. No pun intended, blockchain simply means a chain of blocks using hash to link between two blocks.
2. A simple block itself, typically has 3 parts. Its current hash, some type of value, and the hash of the previous block. See illustration in figure 4 to get a visual idea of how it would look like.
3. A popular algorithm being used by cryptocurrencies such as Bitcoin is called the Proof of Work and can be tweaked in how coins are mined in a particular cryptocurrency. Proof of Work provides the needed security and has been proven to work pretty well so far with the case of Bitcoin for example.

Based on the fundamentals above, below is a simple cryptocurrency implementation using blockchain.

```swift
import Foundation
import UIKit
import CommonCrypto

/// Simple transaction.
struct Transaction: Codable {
    let sender: String
    let recipient: String
    let amount: Int
}

/// Simple block.
struct Block: Codable {
    let proof: Int
    let index: Int
    let timestamp: Date
    let transactions: [Transaction]
    let previousHash: Data

    func hash() -> Data {
        let encoder = JSONEncoder()
        let data = try! encoder.encode(self)
        return data.sha256()
    }

    func description() -> String {
        let json = try! JSONEncoder().encode(self)
        return String(data: json, encoding: .utf8)!
    }
}

extension Data {
```

```swift
    func sha256() -> Data {
        guard let result = NSMutableData(length:
Int(CC_SHA256_DIGEST_LENGTH)) else {
            fatalError("Failed to create SHA256 Digest.")
        }
        CC_SHA256((self as NSData).bytes, CC_LONG(self.count),
result.mutableBytes.assumingMemoryBound(to: UInt8.self))
        return result as Data
    }

    func hexDigest() -> String {
        return self.map({String(format: "%02x", $0)}).joined()
    }
}

/// Simple blockchain class.
class Blockchain {
    /// Initial empty list of transactions.
    private var currentTransactions = [Transaction]()

    /// Initial empty list of blocks in the blockchain.
    var chain = [Block]()

    init() {
        addBlock(proof: 10, previousHash: "1".data(using: .utf8))
    }

    /// Get the last block in the chain.
    ///
    /// - Returns: Last block in the chain.
    func lastBlock() -> Block {
        guard let block = chain.last else {
            fatalError("Chain should at least have one block created
during init.")
        }
        return block
```

```
    }

    /// Creates and add block to chain.
    ///
    /// - Parameters:
    ///    - proof: Block proof.
    ///    - previousHash: Block previous hash.
    /// - Returns: Block created and added to the chain.
    @discardableResult func addBlock(proof: Int, previousHash: Data?
= nil) -> Block {
        let hash: Data
        if let previousHash = previousHash {
            hash = previousHash
        } else {
            hash = lastBlock().hash()
        }

        let block = Block(proof: proof,
                          index: (chain.count + 1),
                          timestamp: Date(),
                          transactions: currentTransactions,
                          previousHash: hash)

        currentTransactions = []

        chain.append(block)

        return block
    }

    /// Creates and add transaction.
    ///
    /// - Parameters:
    ///    - sender: Name of sender.
    ///    - recipient: Name of recipient.
    ///    - amount: Transaction amount.
```

```
/// - Returns: Index of the block that will hold this
transaction.
    @discardableResult func addTransactions(sender: String,
recipient: String, amount: Int) -> Int {
        let transaction = Transaction(sender: sender, recipient:
recipient, amount: amount)
        currentTransactions.append(transaction)
        return lastBlock().index + 1
    }


    // Simple Proof of Work algorithm.


    /// Validates the proof.
    ///
    /// - Parameters:
    ///    - lastProof: Previous proof.
    ///    - proof: Current proof.
    /// - Returns: (true) if hash(lastProof, proof) contains 4
leading zeroes. (false) otherwise.
    class func validProof(lastProof: Int, proof: Int) -> Bool {
        guard let guess = String("\(lastProof)\(proof)").data(using:
.utf8) else {
            fatalError("Unable to convert lastProof and proof into
UTF8 data")
        }
        let guess_hash = guess.sha256().hexDigest()
        print("validProof guess_hash = \(guess_hash)")
        return guess_hash.prefix(4) == "0000"
    }


    /// Find a proof that is a valid proof.
    ///
    /// - Parameter lastProof: Previous proof.
    /// - Returns: Valid proof.
    class func proofOfWork(lastProof: Int) -> Int {
        print("proofOfWork lastProof = \(lastProof)")
```

```swift
        var proof: Int = 0
        while !validProof(lastProof: lastProof, proof: proof) {
            print("proofOfWork proof = \(proof)")
            proof += 1
        }
        return proof
    }
}


/// Simple blockchain server.
class BlockchainServer {
    let blockchain = Blockchain()

    /// Creates and add a new transaction into the blockchain
transactions.
    ///
    /// - Parameters:
    ///    - sender: Sender name.
    ///    - recipient: Recipient name.
    ///    - amount: Block amount.
    /// - Returns: Index of the block that will hold this
transaction.
    func send(sender: String, recipient: String, amount: Int) -> Int
{
        return blockchain.addTransactions(sender: sender, recipient:
recipient, amount:amount)
    }

    /// Mines for coins.
    ///
    /// - Parameters:
    ///    - recipient: Recipient name.
    ///    - completion: Optional closure with the new block.
    func mine(recipient: String, completion: ((Block) -> Void)?) {
        DispatchQueue.global(qos: .default).async {
            // Run proof of work algorithm to find the next proof.
```

```swift
            let lastProof = self.blockchain.lastBlock().proof
            let proof = Blockchain.proofOfWork(lastProof: lastProof)

            // Receive a reward for finding the proof.
            // The sender is "0" to signify that this block has mined
a new coin.
            self.blockchain.addTransactions(sender: "0", recipient:
recipient, amount: 1)

            // Create and add the new block to the chain.
            let block = self.blockchain.addBlock(proof: proof)

            DispatchQueue.main.async {
                completion?(block)
            }
        }
    }


    /// Access the blockchain.
    ///
    /// - Returns: Array of blocks in blockchain.
    func chain() -> [Block] {
        return blockchain.chain
    }
}

// Test the blockchain implementation by mining for coins!

let server = BlockchainServer()

func updateChain() {
    let chain = server.chain()
    var text = "chain:\n"
    for block in chain {
        text.append(block.description() + "\n")
    }
```

```
    print("\(#function) --> \(text)")
}

func sendTransaction(amount: Int) {
    let index = server.send(sender: "me", recipient: "someone",
amount: amount)
    print("Transaction added to block \(index)")
    updateChain()
}

func mineForCoin(completion: ((Block) -> Void)?) {
    let startTime = CACurrentMediaTime()
    print("Mining ...")

    server.mine(recipient: "me") { (block) in
        print("***** New block forged, it took \(CACurrentMediaTime()
- startTime) seconds")
        print("\(block.description())")
        updateChain()
        completion?(block)
    }
}

updateChain()

sendTransaction(amount: 3)
sendTransaction(amount: 5)
sendTransaction(amount: 1)

mineForCoin { (block) in
}
```

There you have it, a simple implementation of a cryptocurrency written in Swift.

Can you guess how long it will take to find a coin with the current implementation? Does the speed of your machine matter?

Hint: Look at the `validProof` method. What happens if you change this line ...

```
guess_hash.prefix(4) == "0000"
```

... to ...

```
guess_hash.prefix(2) == "00"
```

... ?

Hashing is a one-way street to create a digital signature of a piece of data. I will not cover the motivation for hashing and purpose in this book. I highly recommend learning about hash as you will probably run into it here and there as a software engineer.

This all boils down to probability and statistics. The higher number of characters the valid proof requires, the longer it will take for the algorithm to find a match. For the purposes of testing, you can shorten the prefix to a much shorter value and do not forget to match the hex value to meet the new string length.

What other strategies might you use here and why? Let me know by sending me feedback!

There are more interesting topics you can learn in regards to blockchain like Consensus, Smart Contracts, etc. Blockchain continues to evolve, maybe you will discover something in this domain as you get your hands dirty implementing and working on blockchain.

If you like my method of writing and teaching, let me know what other topics you would like me to cover by sending me feedback.

Determining time complexity, big O Notation

In this chapter, we will cover the basics of big O Notation.

Do not be too concerned, if you do not know how to implement these algorithms and also not be able to calculate time complexity correctly at this time. The ones that I think are most difficult to calculate are the ones that use recursion. But that's just me!

In these examples, my goal is to explain them as simple as possible to help you gain a good starting point.

```
// Constant time
// O(1)
// We like constant time because it is predictable.

if 1 > 0 {
    print("yup")
}
```

Also, if a problem has a fixed set of parameters or values, even though the value may seem large, it is also considered constant. Sometimes, these parameters or constraints are hints to achieving the expected time complexity for the problem!

For example, if a problem notes that the length is fixed at 2,000, performing a loop that is fixed at 2,000 is also considered constant time.

```
// Constant time, it will always loop 2000 times regardless of the
input size or length
// O(1)
let n = 2000
for i in 1...2000 {
    // do something
}


// O(n)

let n = 12345
for i in 0 ... n {
    // do something n times
}

// O(n^2)
// slower than O(n) by a lot

for i in 0 ... n {
    for j in 0 ... n {
        // do something n^2 times
    }
}
```

These are basic concepts of big O. There are also concepts such as O(n log n) for algorithms such as merge sort.

We will not cover big O in depth in this book, but it is encouraged for you to get an understanding and have respect for time complexity as it directly affects your code and interview performance. You will also be judged harshly if you use brute force to solve your interview problems.

If you have a good memory, you might want to spend some time to memorize the time complexity for the more complex algorithms and hopefully one day, learn to calculate big O for an algorithm without memorization.

Determining space complexity

Another thing you will need to determine or calculate is the space complexity of an algorithm.

For example, if you used a queue or stack in your algorithm, then the space complexity is usually $O(n)$.

What you really want to strive for, just like Big O, is $O(1)$, which is constant space.

However, in most cases, a better time complexity is always preferred than a better space complexity. If you have to sacrifice one to achieve another, always attempt to find the best time complexity to solve a problem.

If you are using recursion, the calculation becomes a little tricky. For example, if you are using recursion to find something in a BST, then the space complexity is $O(h)$, where h is the height of the tree.

If you are able to use pointers in lieu of a stack or queue to solve a problem, you can reduce your space from $O(n)$ to $O(1)$ as long as you keep the time complexity the same or better.

In the interview questions section, I will provide the time and space complexities for the algorithms used to solve each problem. In some cases, I will showcase multiple possible algorithms with varying time and space complexities for learning purposes.

Common Interview Questions

In this section, we will cover the following problems that I personally have experienced in interviews, from talking to other folks, and also administering them. Start with a few easy ones, then mix it up by grouping them in a more logical order based on relations and similarities of the problems from each other.

- Fibonacci (the 3 ways)

- FizzBuzz (learn about mod operator)

- Reverse linked list

- Valid Parentheses

- Remove minimum characters to make valid parentheses (learn about stacks)

- TwoSum (dynamic programming)

- ThreeSum (more dynamic programming)

- Is Palindrome

- Longest Palindromic Substring

- Text justified (even more dynamic programming)

- Maximum Contiguous Sum

- Boggle (using trie and queue)

- Breadth First Search

- Depth First Search

- Shortest Path (Dijkstra's algorithm)

- Is valid Binary Search Tree

- Invert Binary Tree

- Numpad letter combinations

What is this Dynamic Programming?

You can search the internet for "dynamic programming" and get a definition. The best sentence to summarize what it is comes from Wikipedia.

https://en.wikipedia.org/wiki/Dynamic_programming

"Dynamic programming is a method for solving a complex problem by breaking it down into a collection of simpler subproblems, solving for each just once, and storing their solutions – ideally using a memory-based data structure."

Basically, breaking a complex problem into smaller parts and solving the smaller parts individually, then using it to ultimately figure out the final solution/answer.

Fibonacci

Difficulty: Easy

In math, Fibonacci is a classic and frequently show up in interviews.

Fibonacci can be solved 3 ways; recursive, iterative, and memoize.

```
// Recursive approach
// Time O(2^n)
// Space O(n)
func fibonacciRecursive (n: Int) -> Int {
    if n == 0 {
        return 0
    }
    if n == 1 {
        return 1
    }
    return fibonacciRecursive(n: n - 1) + fibonacciRecursive(n: n -
2)
}

let test1 = fibonacciRecursive(n: 10)

// Iterative approach
// Time O(n)
// Space O(1)
func fibonacciIterative (n: Int) -> Int {
    if n == 0 {
        return 0
    }
    if n == 1 {
        return 1
```

```
    }

    var sum = 1
    var previous = 0

    for _ in 2 ... n {
        let newSum = sum + previous
        previous = sum
        sum = newSum
    }
    return sum
}

let test2 = fibonacciIterative(n: 2)
let test3 = fibonacciIterative(n: 10)

// memoize, using a dictionary as the secret sauce to improve the
recursive performance
// Time O(n)
// Space O(n), due to the dictionary used
var map = [0: 0, 1: 1]
func fibonacciMemoize(n: Int) -> Int {
    if let value = map[n] {
        return value
    } else {
        let f = fibonacciMemoize(n: n - 1) + fibonacciMemoize(n: n -
2)
        map[n] = f
        return f
    }
}

let test4 = fibonacciMemoize(n: 2)
let test5 = fibonacciMemoize(n: 10)
let test6 = fibonacciMemoize(n: 1)
```

```
// performance test
//let performanceRecursive = fibonacciRecursive(n: 60)
//let performanceMemoize = fibonacciMemoize(n: 60)
//let performanceIterative = fibonacciIterative(n: 60)
```

Comments and observation

If you uncomment the lines under performance test, start with the recursive function then go grab a cup of coffee as it will take a while (unless you have an amazing computer).

After the recursive function completes, comment that line out then uncomment the memoize function. Notice how much faster this one computes over the recursive way that you don't even need a scientific way to measure, just through raw observation.

Hopefully this simple comparison of different time complexities shows the value of understanding time complexity and in particular, the Big O.

In a nutshell, 2^n is much slower than **n** for a large number, **n**.

For your interview, know that there are 3 ways, and I recommend solving using iterative. Play it by ear, ask questions from your interviewer and figure out which answer they want to see.

Also, the above return type is **Int**, so you may overflow and error out if you attempt a higher number.

FizzBuzz

Difficulty: Easy

FizzBuzz is another popular interview question. You will be surprised how many candidates actually fail this despite being one of the easier questions.

The magic to this is with the mod operator (%). Some basics, search the internet for detailed explanation.

5 % 3 = 2

6 % 3 = 0 // hint: Fizz!

```
// FizzBuzz
// Write a function that prints the numbers from 1 to n.
// But for multiples of 3, print "Fizz" instead.
// For multiples of 5, print "Buzz" instead.
// For multiples of both 3 and 5, print "FizzBuzz" instead.
// Example series for n = 16
// 1 2 Fizz 4 Buzz Fizz 7 8 Fizz Buzz 11 Fizz 13 14 FizzBuzz 16
//
// Time O(n)
// Space O(1)

func fizzBuzz (n: Int) -> String {
    var results = ""
    if n == 0 {
        return results
    }

    for i in 1 ... n {
```

```
        if i % 3 == 0 && i % 5 == 0 { // Why do we check this first
before the other conditions?
            results += " FizzBuzz"
        } else if i % 3 == 0 {
            results += " Fizz"
        } else if i % 5 == 0 {
            results += " Buzz"
        } else {
            results += " \(i)"
        }
    }
    return results
}

let test1 = fizzBuzz(n: 31)
print(test1)
```

Reverse Linked List

Difficulty: Easy

Linked list in general is quite popular in interviews. Naturally, it is highly likely you will be asked to reverse a **linked list**.

The trick is in handling reversing the next node reference/pointer/that-arrow-thing-you-visually-depict while you are traversing the **linked list** to be efficient and not have to do another loop.

```
/// Reverse a linked list
///
/// Time O(n)
/// Space O(1)
/// - Parameter root: The root node of a linked list.
/// - Returns: The new root node of the reversed linked list.
func reverseLinkedList (root: Node?) -> Node? {
    if root == nil {
        return nil
    }

    // then, traverse the linked list and store them in the stack
    var currentNode: Node? = root
    var previousNode: Node?
    while currentNode != nil {
        let next = currentNode!.next
        currentNode!.next = previousNode
        previousNode = currentNode
        currentNode = next
    }
```

```
    return previousNode
}

var reversedNode = reverseLinkedList(root: root)
// test the linked list by printing them in the new order
print("printing a linked list that was reversed ...")
while reversedNode?.next != nil {
    print(reversedNode?.value ?? "unknown")
    reversedNode = reversedNode?.next!
}
print(reversedNode?.value ?? "unknown")
print("... done printing linked list")
```

Valid Parentheses

Difficulty: Easy

Given a string, determine if the string has valid matching open and close parentheses.

For example:

"((abc))" is valid

"(abc))" is not valid

"((((((()))))))" is valid

"(((((((()))))))" is not valid

"()()()()" is valid

"()((())())" is valid

"))((" is not valid

```
// Strategy
// We can use a stack to keep track if the string has valid open and
close parentheses.
// This takes up O(n) space.
// We can further reduce the space complexity by simply using a
counter.
// The space is now constant, which reduces the space complexity to
O(1).
// For every open parenthesis, we +1. For every close parenthesis we
-1.
// If we ever encounter a situation where the counter is less than 0,
it is impossible for that string to ever be valid.
// In this condition, we return false.
//
```

```swift
// Time O(n)
// Space O(1)

func isValidParentheses(text: String) -> Bool {
    guard !text.isEmpty else { return true }

    var numOfOpenParenthesis = 0

    for c in text {
        if c == "(" {
            numOfOpenParenthesis += 1
        } else if c == ")" {
            if numOfOpenParenthesis == 0 {
                return false
            } else {
                numOfOpenParenthesis -= 1
            }
        }
    }

    if numOfOpenParenthesis == 0 {
        return true
    } else {
        return false
    }
}

// let's test!
let test1 = "(a)"
let test2 = "((bba()"
let test3 = "(((ew)))"
let test4 = "(as)((bqw))"
let test5 = "(("
let test6 = ")("
let test7 = "(((((((())))))))"
let test8 = "((((((((())))))))"
```

```
let test9 = "()()()()()()"
let test10 = "()((())())"

print(isValidParentheses(text: test1)) // true
print(isValidParentheses(text: test2)) // false
print(isValidParentheses(text: test3)) // true
print(isValidParentheses(text: test4)) // true
print(isValidParentheses(text: test5)) // false
print(isValidParentheses(text: test6)) // false
print(isValidParentheses(text: test7)) // true
print(isValidParentheses(text: test8)) // false
print(isValidParentheses(text: test9)) // true
print(isValidParentheses(text: test10)) // true
```

You could also solve this problem using a stack. However, for this problem, that would be overkill. Feel free to attempt that to get comfortable using stacks to solve problems!

Remove minimum characters to make valid parentheses

Difficulty: Medium

Progressing from the previous problem that also involved solving for valid parentheses, we now use a stack to build our algorithm to solve in acceptable time complexity.

```
// Given a String text, remove the minimum number of characters to
make the parentheses valid.
//
// For example:
// text = "())", output = "()"
// text = "))((", output = ""
// text = "jo(h(n()ng)oi", output = "joh(n()ng)oi" OR "jo(hn()ng)oi"
OR "jo(h(n)ng)oi"
//
// Time O(n)
// Space O(n), because of the stack

func minimumCharacters(text: String) -> String {
    guard !text.isEmpty else { return text }

    var chars = [Character](text)
    var stack = [(Character, Int)]()

    for i in chars.indices {
        if chars[i] == "(" {
            stack.append((chars[i], i))
        } else if chars[i] == ")" {
            if stack.count > 0 {
```

```swift
                if stack[stack.endIndex - 1].0 == "(" {
                    stack.removeLast()
                } else {
                    stack.append((chars[i], i))
                }
            } else {
                stack.append((chars[i], i))
            }
        }
    }


    let indexes = stack.map { $0.1 }

    for i in indexes.reversed() {
        chars.remove(at: i)
    }


    return String(chars)
}
```

```
// Let's test!

let test1 = "())"
let test2 = "(a)a)"
let test3 = "(a"
let test4 = "a)"
let test5 = "(((()((())))))))"
let test6 = "()))))))"
let test7 = "a())"
let test8 = "))(("
let test9 = "jo(h(n()ng)oi"

print(minimumCharacters(text: test1))
print(minimumCharacters(text: test2))
print(minimumCharacters(text: test3))
print(minimumCharacters(text: test4))
print(minimumCharacters(text: test5))
print(minimumCharacters(text: test6))
print(minimumCharacters(text: test7))
print(minimumCharacters(text: test8))
print(minimumCharacters(text: test9))
```

TwoSum

Difficulty: Easy

The trick to this problem is to use some math, basically, whatever number you subtract from the sum, you should be able to use a **hash map** aka Swift **Dictionary** to manage finding the pair efficiently.

```
// TwoSum problem
// Given an array of numbers (at least 2), find the two number pairs
that equal to a given sum.
// For example.
// [2, 6, 9, 5, 10, -7]
// The pair for a sum of 15 is [9, 6]

func twoSum (numbers: [Int], sum: Int) -> [Int]? {
    if numbers.count > 1 { // no harm checking if we can even do this
        var map: [Int: Int] = [:]
        for num in numbers {
            let complement = sum - num
            if let other = map[complement] { // hey, this is cheating
:-)
                return [num, other]
            } else {
                map[num] = num // didn't find it in the map, let's
add it!
            }
        }
    }
    return nil
}
```

```
// let's test!

let test = [2, 6, 9, 5, 10, -7]
let result1 = twoSum(numbers: test, sum: 15) // returns [9, 6]
let result2 = twoSum(numbers: test, sum: 3) // returns [-7, 10]
let result3 = twoSum(numbers: test, sum: 22) // returns nil

Time O(n)
Space O(n), where n is the space taken by the dictionary
```

ThreeSum

Difficulty: Medium

If you just came from the TwoSum problem, how about solving for
ThreeSum.

```
// ThreeSum problem
// Given an array of numbers (at least 3), find the two number pairs
that equal to a given sum.
// For example.
// [2, 6, 9, 5, 10, -7]
// The pair for a sum of 24 is [9, 5, 10]
// We could do brute force and come up with a O(n^3) answer, but we
can certainly do better ~ O(n log n)

func ThreeSum (numbers: [Int], sum: Int) -> [Int]? {
    if numbers.count > 2 {
        // cannot escape going through the numbers once in one
dimension
        // probably helpful if I could get the index
        // j and k will traverse from the left and right most end of
the array and meet in the middle

        for (i, _) in numbers.enumerated() {
            var j = 1
            var k = numbers.count - 1
            while j < k {
                print("\(i) \(j) \(k) ")
                let a = numbers[i]
                let b = numbers[j]
                let c = numbers[k]
                if (a + b + c) == sum {
```

```
                    if i != j && i != k { // not so fast, you also
have to check for non overlap before declaring victory
                        return [a, b, c]
                    }
                }

                // don't forget to increment and decrement
                j += 1
                k -= 1
            }
        }
    }
    return nil
}

// let's test!
let test = [2, 6, 9, 5, 10, -7]
let result1 = ThreeSum(numbers: test, sum: 21) // returns [2, 9, 10]
let result2 = ThreeSum(numbers: test, sum: 24) // returns [5, 9, 10]
let result3 = ThreeSum(numbers: test, sum: 25) // returns [6, 9, 10]
let result4 = ThreeSum(numbers: test, sum: 26) // returns nil
let result5 = ThreeSum(numbers: test, sum: 6) // returns nil
```

Is Palindrome

Difficulty: Easy

```
// Given a string, determine if it is a palindrome.
// A palindrome is where the string spelled in either direction is
the same.
//
// For example:
// "dad" is a palindrome
// "madam" is a palindrome
// "a" is a palindrome
// "bad" is not a palindrome. The reverse is spelled "dab".
// Assume the string has no spaces.
//
// Strategy
// Use pointers to iterate from the beginning and last character,
until it meets in the middle.
// Time O(n)
// Space O(1), using pointers saves space!

func isPalindrome(_ text: String) -> Bool {
    guard !text.isEmpty else { return true }

    let text = [Character](text) // copy to an array of Characters
    var i = 0
    var j = text.count - 1

    while i < j {
        defer {
            i += 1
            j -= 1
        }
```

```swift
        if text[i] != text[j] {
            return false
        }
    }

    return true
}

func printResults(_ input: String) {
    print("\(input) is \(isPalindrome(input))")
}

printResults("dad")
printResults("bad")
printResults("a")
printResults("bb")
printResults("ccc")
printResults("madam")
```

Longest Palindromic Substring

Difficulty: Medium

Progressing from the previous problem, where we solve if a string is a palindrome, here we have a harder problem involving palindromes with a twist!

```
// Given a string, find the longest palindromic substring.
//
// For example:
//
// text: babad, results: aba, OR bab
// text: abba, results: abba
// text: abc, results can either be a, b OR, c
//
// Strategy
// Think of the sub problem, we can easily determine the longest
palindrome from the center of any given string.
// Write a sub function to determine the longest length of a
palindrome from any given index in the string.
// Then, iterate through the string to get the middle indexes.
// Time O(n^2)
// Space O(1)

func longestPalindrome(_ text: String) -> String {
    func expandFromMiddle(_ s: [Character], left: Int, right: Int) ->
Int {
        var left = left
        var right = right

        while (left >= 0 && right < s.count && s[left] == s[right]) {
            left -= 1
```

```swift
            right += 1
        }

        return right - left - 1
    }

    guard !text.isEmpty else { return text }
    if text.count == 1 { return text }

    let s = [Character](text)
    var start = 0
    var end = 0

    for i in 0..<s.count {
        let len1 = expandFromMiddle(s, left: i, right: i)
        let len2 = expandFromMiddle(s, left: i, right: i + 1)
        let len = max(len1, len2)

        if len > (end - start) {
            start = i - (len - 1) / 2
            end = i + len / 2
        }
    }

    return String(s[start...end])
}

func printResults(_ text: String) {
    print("\(text), results is \(longestPalindrome(text))")
}

printResults("abba")
printResults("abc")
printResults("babad")
printResults("cbbd")
printResults("qiruqhrfkwafhajafsh")
```

Text justification

Difficulty: Hard

```
// Text justification
// Given a string of words and a max length, L, format the text such
that each line has exactly L characters and is fully left and right
justified.
// Restrictions:
// You need to fit as many words in every line.
// You are not allowed to split a word and put them in next line.
// Pad extra spaces if needed so that each line has L characters.
// Extra spaces between words should be distributed as evenly as
possible.
// Example ...
// words = ["This", "is", "an", "example", "of", "text",
"justification."]
// line length = 16
// result =
// ["This     is     an",
// "example  of text",
// "justification.   "]
//

func textJustification (words: [String], maxLength: Int) -> [String]?
{
    var results = [String]() // store the results of each line

    if words.count == 0 || maxLength == 0 {
        return results
    }

    var lineCharacterCount = 0 // counter to keep track of number of
characters per line
```

```swift
    var lineIndex = 0 // index tracker to start each new line from
the words array

    for (i, word) in words.enumerated() {
        lineCharacterCount += word.count + 1
        if lineCharacterCount >= maxLength {
            let beginLineIndex = lineIndex
            let endLineIndex = i - 1
            lineIndex = i

            // find the leftover space
            let count = lineCharacterCount - (word.count + 2)

            lineCharacterCount = 0 // reset to ZERO
            lineCharacterCount += word.count + 1 // begin counting
for the next line

            // calculate the leftover to fill with spaces
            var leftover = maxLength - count
            print("leftover = \(leftover)")

            // try to evenly distribute the spaces
            let numberOfGaps = endLineIndex - beginLineIndex
            print("numberOfGaps = \(numberOfGaps)")
            var extraSpaces = 0
            if numberOfGaps > 0 {
                extraSpaces = leftover / numberOfGaps
            }
            print("extraSpacesPerGap = \(extraSpaces)")
            leftover = leftover - (extraSpaces * numberOfGaps)
            print("leftover after = \(leftover)")

            // construct the line left and right justified
            var text = ""
            for word in words[beginLineIndex..<endLineIndex] {
                text.append(word)
```

```swift
                text.append(" ")
                if leftover > 0 {
                    leftover -= 1
                    text.append(" ")
                }
                let spaces = String(repeating: " ", count:
extraSpaces)
                text.append(spaces)
            }
            text.append(words[endLineIndex])
            print("line text = \(text)")
            results.append(text)
        }


        // handle last line
        if i == words.endIndex - 1 {
            let beginLineIndex = lineIndex
            let endLineIndex = i

            var text = ""
            for word in words[beginLineIndex..<endLineIndex] {
                text.append(word)
                text.append(" ")
            }
            text.append(words[endLineIndex])
            results.append(text)
        }

    }
    return results
}


// let's test!
let test1 = ["This", "is", "an", "example", "of", "text",
"justification."]
let result1 = textJustification(words: test1, maxLength: 16)
print(result1!)
```

```
let test2 = ["This", "is", "an", "example", "of", "text",
"justification."]
let result2 = textJustification(words: test1, maxLength: 8)
print(result2!)

let test3 = ["This", "is", "an", "example", "of", "text",
"justification."]
let result3 = textJustification(words: test1, maxLength: 20)
print(result3!)
```

Maximum Contiguous Sum

Difficulty: Medium (if you just return the sum), Hard (if you also return the subarray)

The secret to this is to think about the sum of the previous number while traversing the number **array** and compare it to the current number you are at.

$k - 1$ vs k

In addition, we use a variable to track the max sum ever met, and this is a growing number as it iterates through the numbers. *Hint: See a trend!?*

Personally, I don't use the word "contiguous" much in day to day, so I had to look up the definition.

con-tig-u-ous
adjective
- Sharing a common border; touching
- Next or together in a sequence

```
// Maximum Contiguous Sum
// Given an array of numbers, find the contiguous subarray that has
the largest sum.
// For example
// Given an array, [-2,1,-3,4,-1,2,1,-5,4]
```

```swift
// Contiguous subarray with the larget sum is [4, -1, 2, 1] and the
sum is 6

func maxContiguousSumSubArray (numbers: [Int]) -> [Int]? {
    if numbers.count == 1 { // why bother to even run through the
code, quick answer O(1)
        return numbers
    }

    if numbers.count > 1 {
        // trackers to compare
        var currentSum: Int = numbers[0]
        var max = numbers[0] // the secret sauce

        // keep track of where the subarray begins and end
        var startIndex = 0
        var endIndex = 0

        for (index, num) in numbers.enumerated() {
            if num > max {
                startIndex = index // figure out the startIndex
            }
            let newSum = currentSum + num

            currentSum = Swift.max(newSum, num)
            let newMax = Swift.max(max, currentSum) // this number
always grows. Hint: See a trend!?
            if newMax > max {
                endIndex = index // figure out the endIndex
            }
            max = newMax
        }

        let subarray = numbers[startIndex ... endIndex].compactMap {
$0 } // there is something funky about array slices, use flatMap to
flatten the elements into a legit array of numbers
```

```
        return subarray
    }
    return nil
}


// let's test!
let test1 = [-2, 1, -3, 4, -1, 2, 1, -5, 4]
let result1 = maxContiguousSumSubArray(numbers: test1) // prints [4,
-1, 2, 1]
let sum1 = result1?.reduce(0, { x, y in
    x + y
})


let test2 = [-2, -1, -3, -4,-1, -2, -1, -5, -4]
let result2 = maxContiguousSumSubArray(numbers: test2) // prints [-1]


let test3 = [5]
let result3 = maxContiguousSumSubArray(numbers: test3) // prints [5]


let test4 = [5, -5]
let result4 = maxContiguousSumSubArray(numbers: test4) // prints [5]


let test5 = [-5, 5]
let result5 = maxContiguousSumSubArray(numbers: test5) // prints [5]
```

Boggle

Difficulty: Hard

There are probably a few ways to solve this. Taking from the lesson you have learned in the book, we will use a **trie** as our magic sauce.

If you forgot what a **trie** is, go back up a few chapters and revisit **tries** and practice building one from scratch.

```
// Boggle, find all possible words in a board of characters
// Given a dictionary, and a M x N board with a character in each
cell, find all possible words that can be formed by a sequence of
adjacent characters.
// We can move in any of the 8 adjacent characters but a word should
not have multiple instances of same cell.
// Hint: We will use a Trie to solve for this.

// create a trie
class TrieNode {
    var letter: Character
    var isWord: Bool
    var children = [Character: TrieNode]()

    init (letter le: Character, isWord iw: Bool) {
        self.letter = le
        self.isWord = iw
    }
}

class Trie {
    var root: TrieNode = TrieNode(letter: "\0", isWord: false)
```

```swift
func insertWord (word: String) {
    let wordLength = word.count
    var currentNode: TrieNode? = root
    var letterCounter = 0

    for letter in word {
        letterCounter = letterCounter + 1

        let isWord = letterCounter == wordLength ? true : false

        if currentNode!.children[letter] == nil {
            currentNode!.children[letter] = TrieNode(letter:
letter, isWord: isWord)
        }
        currentNode = currentNode!.children[letter]
    }
}

func find (key: String) -> String? {
    let keyLength = key.count

    var currentNode: TrieNode? = self.root
    var characterCount = 0

    for character in key {
        currentNode = currentNode!.children[character]

        if currentNode == nil {
            return nil
        }

        characterCount = characterCount + 1

        if characterCount == keyLength && currentNode!.isWord ==
true {
```

```
                return key
            }
        }

        return nil
    }
}

// test your trie
var trie: Trie = Trie()
trie.insertWord(word: "nicolas")
trie.insertWord(word: "nighthawk")
trie.find(key: "nicolas")
trie.find(key: "john")
trie.find(key: "nighthawk")
trie.insertWord(word: "lilian")
trie.find(key: "lilian")

// solving Boggle using a trie

// boggle 2D array
let boggle = [["T", "F", "F"],
              ["U", "H", "K"],
              ["N", "S", "I"]
]

// first add the words to the trie
var wordsTrie = Trie()
wordsTrie.insertWord(word: "THIS")
wordsTrie.insertWord(word: "IS")
wordsTrie.insertWord(word: "FUN")
wordsTrie.insertWord(word: "STUFF")

// once we loaded up our trie with words, implement the find function
func findWords (boggle: [[String]]) -> [String]? {
    let rows = boggle.count
```

```swift
let cols = boggle[0].count
var words = [String]()
var queue = [(x: Int, y: Int, prefix: String, node: TrieNode)]()

// setup the initial queue
for (i, col) in boggle.enumerated() {
    for (j, char) in col.enumerated() {
        if let node = wordsTrie.root.children[Character(char)] {
            queue.append((x: i, y: j, prefix: char, node: node))
        }
    }
}

while !queue.isEmpty {
    let node = queue.removeFirst()
    for (dx, dy) in [(1,0), (1, -1), (0, -1), (-1, -1), (-1, 0),
(-1, 1), (0, 1), (1, 1)] { // this one is funky, basically go all 8
possible directions
        let x2 = node.x + dx
        let y2 = node.y + dy

        if x2 >= 0 && x2 < cols && y2 >= 0 && y2 < rows { // off
course, you want to make sure you keep within the boggle board
            let char2 = boggle[x2][y2]
            let prefix2 = node.prefix + char2
            if let node2 = node.node.children[Character(char2)] {
                if node2.isWord == true {
                    words.append(prefix2)
                }
                queue.append((x: x2, y: y2, prefix: prefix2,
node: node2))
            }
        }
    }
}
```

```
    return words
}

findWords(boggle: boggle) // returns ["IS", "FUN", "THIS"]
```

Comments and observation

The time complexity of solving that using a trie and a queue looks to be $O(n^2)$. Can you find a better solution for this in Swift? (email me!)

Tip: This is a great cheat to use against boggle games!

Breadth First Search (BFS)

Difficulty: Medium

The secret to **BFS**, is the use of a **queue** to scan through the nodes/**vertex**/those-dots-that-connect-to-each-other.

This is one of the simplest examples that also tries to solve a problem to represent **BFS**.

```
// Breadth First Search (BFS)
// Simple implementation of BFS
// Given a graph of nodes (directed), find the number of nodes it
will take from one node to another, do not count the starting node
//

class Node {
    var visited = false
    var data: Int
    var neighbors = [Node]()
    // special to count the steps
    var steps = 0

    init (data: Int) {
        self.data = data
    }
}

func bfs(from: Node, to: Node) -> Int {
    var queue = [Node]() // the magic sauce
    queue.append(from) // enqueue
```

```
    while queue.isEmpty == false { // more magic here
        let node = queue.removeFirst() // dequeue

        for neighbor in node.neighbors {
            if neighbor.visited == false {
                neighbor.visited = true
                neighbor.steps = node.steps + 1

                if neighbor.data == to.data {
                    return neighbor.steps // found the destination
                }

                queue.append(neighbor) // enqueue
            }
        }
    }
    return 0
}

// let's test!
let node1 = Node(data: 1)
let node2 = Node(data: 2)
let node3 = Node(data: 3)
let node4 = Node(data: 4)
let node5 = Node(data: 5)
let node6 = Node(data: 6)
let node7 = Node(data: 7)
let node8 = Node(data: 8)
let node9 = Node(data: 9)

// create a graph
node1.neighbors.append(node3)
node1.neighbors.append(node4)
node3.neighbors.append(node5)
node3.neighbors.append(node2)
node3.neighbors.append(node6)
```

```
node2.neighbors.append(node5)
node5.neighbors.append(node7)
node6.neighbors.append(node8)
node8.neighbors.append(node9)

// can you visualize the above graph? See Appendix A.
// Hint: It's OK to use a pen and paper to draw this out!

let result = bfs(from: node1, to: node7) // returns 3
```

Depth First Search (DFS)

Difficulty: Medium

If you just came from **BFS**, **DFS** is similar except it uses a **stack** as its secret sauce.

```
// Depth First Search (DFS)
// Simple implementation of DFS
// Given a directed graph, find the farthest node from a given node.
//

class Node {
    var visited = false
    var data: Int
    var neighbors = [Node]()
    // special to count the steps
    var steps = 0

    init (data: Int) {
        self.data = data
    }
}

// find farthest node using DFS
func dfs (from: Node) -> (Int, Node) {
    var stack = [Node]() // the magic sauce
    stack.append(from) // push

    var longest = 0
    var farthestNode = from

    while stack.isEmpty == false {
```

```
            let node = stack.removeLast() // pop

            for neighbor in node.neighbors {
                neighbor.visited = true
                neighbor.steps = node.steps + 1

                if neighbor.steps > longest {
                    longest = neighbor.steps
                    farthestNode = neighbor
                }

                stack.append(neighbor) // push
            }
    }

    return (longest, farthestNode)
}

// let's test!
let node1 = Node(data: 1)
let node2 = Node(data: 2)
let node3 = Node(data: 3)
let node4 = Node(data: 4)
let node5 = Node(data: 5)
let node6 = Node(data: 6)
let node7 = Node(data: 7)
let node8 = Node(data: 8)
let node9 = Node(data: 9)

// create a graph
node1.neighbors.append(node3)
node1.neighbors.append(node4)
node3.neighbors.append(node5)
node3.neighbors.append(node2)
node3.neighbors.append(node6)
node2.neighbors.append(node5)
```

```
node5.neighbors.append(node7)
node6.neighbors.append(node8)
node8.neighbors.append(node9)

// can you visualize the above graph? See Appendix A.
// Hint: It's OK to use a pen and paper to draw this out!

let result = dfs(from: node1) // returns 4, node9
```

Shortest Path (Dijkstra's algorithm in action!)

Difficulty: Hard

In my opinion, **Dijkstra's** is kinda a modified **BFS**, except fancier and more useful. It uses a **queue** to scan through a **graph**. Very useful in finding shortest path and you can imagine use of this algorithm in maps.

Tip: If the weight of the edges are 1 or undefined, you can use BFS instead since you will simply be incrementing each step by 1.

Borrowing the **graph** we created in an earlier chapter, here's how you find the distance of shortest path between two **vertices**.

```
// Shortest Path using Dijkstra's algorithm
// Given a directed graph, find the shortest path distance between
two vertices
//

class Vertex {
    var key: String?
    var neighbors: [Edge]
    // special distance tracker
    var distance = 0

    init () {
        self.neighbors = [Edge]()
    }

    init (key: String) {
```

```swift
            self.key = key
            self.neighbors = [Edge]()
    }
}


class Edge {
    var neighbor: Vertex
    var weight: Int

    init () {
        self.weight = 0
        self.neighbor = Vertex()
    }
}

class Graph {

    var canvas: [Vertex]
    var isDirected: Bool

    init() {
        self.canvas = [Vertex]()
        self.isDirected = true
    }

    func addVertex (key: String) -> Vertex {
        // create a vertex with the key
        let childVertex: Vertex = Vertex(key: key)

        // add vertex to graph canvas
        canvas.append(childVertex)
        return childVertex
    }

    func addEdge (source: Vertex, neighbor: Vertex, weight: Int) {
        // create a new edge
```

```
let newEdge = Edge()
newEdge.neighbor = neighbor
newEdge.weight = weight
source.neighbors.append(newEdge)

// check for undirected graph
if isDirected == false {
    // create a reverse edge
    let reverseEdge = Edge()
    reverseEdge.neighbor = source
    reverseEdge.weight = weight
    neighbor.neighbors.append(reverseEdge)
}
}


func shortestPathCost (from: Vertex, to: Vertex) -> Int {
    // first, set all the distance to max
    for v in self.canvas {
        v.distance = Int.max
    }

    // set the starting node distance to 0
    from.distance = 0

    var queue = [Vertex]() // magic sauce
    queue.append(from) // enqueue

    while queue.isEmpty == false {
        let vertex = queue.removeFirst() // dequeue

        // scan the edges
        for edge in vertex.neighbors {
            let updatedDistance = edge.weight + vertex.distance
            if updatedDistance < edge.neighbor.distance {
                edge.neighbor.distance = updatedDistance //
update the distance value with the lowest found
```

```
            }
            queue.append(edge.neighbor) // enqueue
        }
    }
    return to.distance
    }
}


// let's test!
let graph = Graph()
let vertex1 = graph.addVertex(key: "G")
let vertex2 = graph.addVertex(key: "H")
let vertex3 = graph.addVertex(key: "A")
let vertex4 = graph.addVertex(key: "C")
let vertex5 = graph.addVertex(key: "Z")
graph.addEdge(source: vertex1, neighbor: vertex2, weight: 5)
graph.addEdge(source: vertex1, neighbor: vertex3, weight: 1)
graph.addEdge(source: vertex1, neighbor: vertex5, weight: 11)
graph.addEdge(source: vertex2, neighbor: vertex4, weight: 1)
graph.addEdge(source: vertex4, neighbor: vertex5, weight: 2)

let result = graph.shortestPathCost(from: vertex1, to: vertex5) //
returns 8
// there are two paths to "Z", one cost 8, one cost 11
```

Is valid Binary Search Tree

Difficulty: Easy

```
// Given a binary tree, determine if it is a valid binary search tree
(BST).
//
// Assume a BST is defined as follows:
//
// The left subtree of a node contains only nodes with keys less than
the node's key.
// The right subtree of a node contains only nodes with keys greater
than the node's key.
// Both the left and right subtrees must also be binary search trees.
//
// Strategy
// We can simply perform a tree traversal for each and every node.
// Then compare the left and right values to satisfy the BST
conditions.
// As you continue to traverse to the subtrees, you will need to set
new upper or lower bound limits to ensure the subtrees satisfy the
BST conditions.
// Time O(n), all nodes are visited and evaluated
// Space O(n), the queue takes up n extra space

class Node {
    var val: Int
    var left: Node?
    var right: Node?

    init(_ value: Int) {
        val = value
    }
}
```

```swift
class Tree {
    var root: Node
    init(_ value: Int) {
        root = Node(value)
    }

    func insert(_ value: Int) {
        var queue = [Node]()
        queue.append(root)

        while !queue.isEmpty {
            let node = queue.removeFirst()

            if node.left == nil {
                node.left = Node(value)
                return
            } else {
                queue.append(node.left!)
            }

            if node.right == nil {
                node.right = Node(value)
                return
            } else {
                queue.append(node.right!)
            }
        }
    }
}


func isValidBST(_ root: Node?) -> Bool {
    guard let root = root else { return true }

    func helper(_ node: Node?, _ lower: Int = Int.min, _ upper: Int =
Int.max) -> Bool {
```

```swift
        guard let node = node else { return true }
        if node.val <= lower {
            return false
        }

        if node.val >= upper {
            return false
        }

        if !helper(node.left, lower, node.val) {
            return false
        }

        if !helper(node.right, node.val, upper) {
            return false
        }

        return true
    }

    return helper(root)
}
```

```
// Let's test!

let tree1 = Tree(10)
tree1.insert(8)
tree1.insert(15)
tree1.insert(3)
tree1.insert(9)
tree1.insert(13)
tree1.insert(16)
print("tree1 results")
print(isValidBST(tree1.root))

let tree2 = Tree(10)
tree2.insert(9)
tree2.insert(15)
tree2.insert(3)
tree2.insert(11)
tree2.insert(13)
tree2.insert(16)
print("tree2 results")
print(isValidBST(tree2.root))

let tree3 = Tree(10)
print("tree3 results")
print(isValidBST(tree3.root))
```

Invert Binary Tree

Difficulty: Easy

This problem gained quite a bit of notoriety when the creator of a popular software platform was rejected at a top tier tech company for failing to invert a binary tree during the interview. I personally use the creator's software and I consider the tool to be important in my software development. I also make this tool a standard in my teams.

If you are curious, search the web for "invert binary tree notoriety" for the scoop!

If you think about the problem a bit, it is an easy problem. It definitely helps if you have seen and solved this problem in the first place ;-)

Here's a visual of what inverting a binary tree would look like.

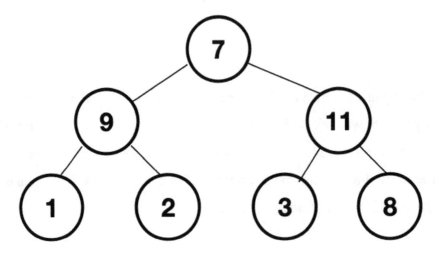

Figure 6. Binary tree

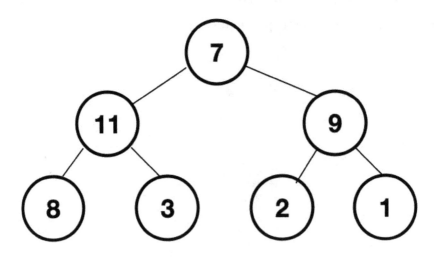

Figure 7. The binary tree after it has been inverted

```
// Strategy
// This is all about your pointer skills!
// Simply swap the left and right child nodes.
// Then recursively travel left, and right, and swapping their left
and right children along the way.
//
// Time O(n)
// Space O(h), height of tree
//
//class Node {
//     var value: Int
//     var left: Node?
//     var right: Node?
//
//     init(value: Int) {
//         self.value = value
//     }
//}

func invertBinaryTree(_ root: Node?) {
    guard let root = root else { return }

    let left = root.left
    root.left = root.right
    root.right = left

    invertBinaryTree(root.left)
    invertBinaryTree(root.right)
}
```

Practice suggestion

Try solving this without referring to the book. Who knows, you might actually encounter this question in one of your interviews and you would be glad that you took up this practice suggestion! ;-)

Numpad letter combinations

Difficulty: Medium

```
// List all possible combinations from a numpad input
//
// The numpad has the following number to letter association
//
// Begin numpad
//     1      2      3
//           abc    def
//     4      5      6
//    ghi    jkl    mno
//     7      8      9
//    pqrs   tuv    wxyz
//.           0
//
// End numpad
//
// For example
// text = "3", output = ["d", "e", "f"]
// text = "35", output = ["dj", "dk", "dl", "ej", "ek", "el", "fj",
"fk", "fl"]
// text = "3412", putput = ["dga", "dgb", "dgc", "dha", "dhb", "dhc",
"dia", "dib", "dic", "ega", "egb", "egc", "eha", "ehb", "ehc", "eia",
"eib", "eic", "fga", "fgb", "fgc", "fha", "fhb", "fhc", "fia", "fib",
"fic"]

// Strategy
// Sometimes it helps to simualte the outputs from inputs of varying
lengths (n)
// Notice a pattern?
// One way to establish a relationship between one number to the next
is a graph like structure
```

```swift
// Let's take "23"
// We can build the graph like so
// 2a -> 3d, 2a -> 3e, 2a -> 3f
// 2b -> 3d, 2b -> 3e, 2b -> 3f
// 2c -> 3d, 2c -> 3e, 2c -> 3f
// Try drawing out the output of "237", what does it look like?
// Now that we know this can be solved using a graph type algorithm,
the most efficient way to traverse all possible nodes is using DFS
(recursively)
// Other sub problem to solve is the access time for each number to
letters.
// here, we can simply create a Dictionary with the numbers (keys)
associated with an array of letters (values).
//
// Time O(nk), n is the length of the string, k is the max possible
letters for each number
// Space O(nk)


func numpad(_ text: String) -> [String] {
    guard !text.isEmpty else { return [] }

    let numpad: [Character: [Character]] = [
        "1": [],
        "2": ["a", "b", "c"],
        "3": ["d", "e", "f"],
        "4": ["g", "h", "i"],
        "5": ["j", "k", "l"],
        "6": ["m", "n", "o"],
        "7": ["p", "q", "r", "s"],
        "8": ["t", "u", "v"],
        "9": ["w", "x", "y", "z"],
        "0": []
    ]

    var results = [String]()
```

```swift
    func helper(_ i: Int, prefix: String) {
        if i == text.count {
            results.append(prefix)
            return
        }


        let char = text[text.index(text.startIndex, offsetBy: i)]

        if let chars = numpad[char] {
            if chars.count == 0 {
                helper(i + 1, prefix: prefix)
            } else {
                for c in chars {
                    helper(i + 1, prefix: prefix + String(c))
                }
            }
        } else {
            results.append("invalid num!")
            return
        }
    }


    helper(0, prefix: "")

    return results
}
print(numpad("3")) // ["d", "e", "f"]

print(numpad("34"))  // ["dg", "dh", "di", "eg", "eh", "ei", "fg",
"fh", "fi"]

print(numpad("3412")) // ["dga", "dgb", "dgc", "dha", "dhb", "dhc",
"dia", "dib", "dic", "ega", "egb", "egc", "eha", "ehb", "ehc", "eia",
"eib", "eic", "fga", "fgb", "fgc", "fha", "fhb", "fhc", "fia", "fib",
"fic"]
```

```
print(numpad("341209")) // ["dgaw", "dgax", "dgay", "dgaz", "dgbw",
"dgbx", "dgby", "dgbz", "dgcw", "dgcx", "dgcy", "dgcz", "dhaw",
"dhax", "dhay", "dhaz", "dhbw", "dhbx", "dhby", "dhbz", "dhcw",
"dhcx", "dhcy", "dhcz", "diaw", "diax", "diay", "diaz", "dibw",
"dibx", "diby", "dibz", "dicw", "dicx", "dicy", "dicz", "egaw",
"egax", "egay", "egaz", "egbw", "egbx", "egby", "egbz", "egcw",
"egcx", "egcy", "egcz", "ehaw", "ehax", "ehay", "ehaz", "ehbw",
"ehbx", "ehby", "ehbz", "ehcw", "ehcx", "ehcy", "ehcz", "eiaw",
"eiax", "eiay", "eiaz", "eibw", "eibx", "eiby", "eibz", "eicw",
"eicx", "eicy", "eicz", "fgaw", "fgax", "fgay", "fgaz", "fgbw",
"fgbx", "fgby", "fgbz", "fgcw", "fgcx", "fgcy", "fgcz", "fhaw",
"fhax", "fhay", "fhaz", "fhbw", "fhbx", "fhby", "fhbz", "fhcw",
"fhcx", "fhcy", "fhcz", "fiaw", "fiax", "fiay", "fiaz", "fibw",
"fibx", "fiby", "fibz", "ficw", "ficx", "ficy", "ficz"]
```

Swift String nuances

I recommend reading up on Apple's documentation on the Swift String before continuing.

https://developer.apple.com/documentation/swift/string

In addition, I recommend reading this page from swift.org.

https://docs.swift.org/swift-book/LanguageGuide/StringsAndCharacters.html

In a nutshell, Swift String is a very important structure in your developer life.

If Swift is your first programming language, you may not notice a particular nuance with how Swift handles strings, in particular, how the String is subscripted.

For example, here is how you would solve for a problem involving a String input simply using Swift String.

```swift
func isPalindromeSwift(_ text: String) -> Bool {
    guard !text.isEmpty else { return true }

    var i = 0
    var j = text.count - 1

    while i < j {
        defer {
```

```
            i += 1
            j -= 1
    }

    if text[text.index(text.startIndex, offsetBy: i)] !=
text[text.index(text.startIndex, offsetBy: j)] {
            return false
    }
  }

    return true
}
```

Notice this ugly thing.

```
if text[text.index(text.startIndex, offsetBy: i)] !=
text[text.index(text.startIndex, offsetBy: j)] {
            return false
    }
```

Now, if we copied the String to an array of Characters, the solution would look like this.

```swift
func isPalindrome(_ text: String) -> Bool {
    guard !text.isEmpty else { return true }

    let text = [Character](text) // easier to work with an array of
characters than a String
    var i = 0
    var j = text.count - 1

    while i < j {
        defer {
            i += 1
            j -= 1
        }

        if text[i] != text[j] {
            return false
        }
    }

    return true
}
```

Now, that ugly block of code earlier, now looks like this.

```
if text[i] != text[j] {
    return false
}
```

I personally think this looks much better and easier to handle, especially when you are going to be dealing with much larger problems.

In Swift, the String type does not have the usual Array-like subscripts. If you have experience with another programming language like Objective-C, Python, Java, or C++, they all support the usual array subscript to access elements in the array.

If it simplifies your approach, you can simply copy the string into an array of characters to gain access to what you may be familiar with. Plus it is much easier to read and manage, and a lot less to type (and get wrong!).

Additionally, you could write a subscript in a String extension that behaves like the good old subscript.

```
extension String {
    subscript(value: Int) -> Character {
        return self[self.index(self.startIndex, offsetBy: value)]
    }
}
```

Now you can simply do this in your algorithm without copying the String into an array of Characters.

```
        if text[i] != text[j] {
            return false
        }
```

Parting words

Congratulations! You have reached the end of the book. Hopefully this book has helped you prepare for your upcoming interview. Let me know how it went.

If you love this book, or it got you that sweet software engineering job, drop me a sweeter review on Amazon!

Here is the link to the book:

https://www.amazon.com/Interviewing-Swift-Algorithms-Structures-engineering-ebook/dp/B01L8DY5H6/ref=sr_1_1?ie=UTF8&qid=1537932779&sr=8-1&keywords=B01L8DY5H6

Good luck and keep practicing!

Appendix A

Implement queue using linked list

Borrowing from the **linked list** example previously, here is how you can implement a **queue** using a **linked list**.

```
/// Linked list node.
class Node {
    var value: Int
    var next: Node?

    init (value: Int, next: Node?) {
        self.value = value
        self.next = next
    }
}

/// A simple queue implementation using a linked list.
class Queue {
    var root: Node?
    var count = 0

    func enqueue (node: Node) {
        if self.root == nil {
            self.root = node
            self.count += 1
        } else {
            var currentNode = self.root!
            while currentNode.next != nil {

                currentNode = currentNode.next!
```

```swift
            }
            currentNode.next = node
            self.count += 1
        }
    }

    func dequeue () -> Node? {
        if self.root == nil {
            return nil
        }

        let node = self.root!
        self.root = node.next
        node.next = nil
        self.count -= 1
        return node
    }

    func printNodes () -> String {
        var results = ""
        if self.root == nil {
            return results
        }

        var currentNode = self.root!
        results += "\(currentNode.value)"
        while currentNode.next != nil {
            currentNode = currentNode.next!
            results += " \(currentNode.value)"
        }
        return results
    }
}

// let's test!
let queue = Queue()
```

146

```
let root3 = Node(value: 5, next: nil)
let second3 = Node(value: 9, next: nil)
let third3 = Node(value: 2, next: nil)
let fourth3 = Node(value: 8, next: nil)
queue.enqueue(node: root3)
queue.enqueue(node: second3)
queue.enqueue(node: third3)
queue.enqueue(node: fourth3)
queue.printNodes() // returns 5 9 2 8
queue.count // returns 4
let de = queue.dequeue()
print("printing value of node that was dequeued =
\(String(describing: de!.value))") // prints 5
queue.printNodes() // returns 9 2 8
queue.count // returns 3
```

Implement stack using linked list

Borrowing from the **linked list** example previously, here is how you can implement a **stack** using a **linked list**.

```
/// Linked list node.
class Node {
    var value: Int
    var next: Node?

    init (value: Int, next: Node?) {
        self.value = value
        self.next = next
    }
}

/// Stack implemented using a linked list.
class Stack {
    var root: Node?
    var count = 0

    func push (node: Node) {
        if self.root == nil {
            self.root = node
            self.count += 1
        } else {
            var currentNode = self.root!
            while currentNode.next != nil {

                currentNode = currentNode.next!
            }
            currentNode.next = node
            self.count += 1
        }
```

```swift
    }

    func pop () -> Node? {
        if self.root == nil {
            return nil
        }

        var currentNode = self.root
        var previousNode: Node?
        while currentNode?.next != nil {
            previousNode = currentNode
            currentNode = currentNode!.next
        }
        previousNode?.next = nil
        self.count -= 1
        return currentNode
    }

    func printNodes () -> String {
        var results = ""
        if self.root == nil {
            return results
        }

        var currentNode = self.root!
        results += "\(currentNode.value)"
        while currentNode.next != nil {
            currentNode = currentNode.next!
            results += " \(currentNode.value)"
        }
        return results
    }
}

// let's test!
let stack = Stack()
```

```
let root4 = Node(value: 5, next: nil)
let second4 = Node(value: 9, next: nil)
let third4 = Node(value: 2, next: nil)
let fourth4 = Node(value: 8, next: nil)
stack.push(node: root4)
stack.push(node: second4)
stack.push(node: third4)
stack.push(node: fourth4)
stack.printNodes() // returns 5 9 2 8
let se = stack.pop()
print("printing value of node that was popped from stack =
\(String(describing: se!.value))") // prints 8
stack.printNodes() // returns 5 9 2
```

Maximum Contiguous Sum

Previously, we showed how to solve for this problem in hard mode. This is one way to solve for the problem and only return the sum.

Hint: You can continue to use the same technic, minus figuring out the start and end indices.

```
// Maximum Contiguous Sum
// Given an array of numbers, find the contiguous subarray that has
the largest sum.
// For example
// Given an array, [-2,1,-3,4,-1,2,1,-5,4]
// Contiguous subarray with the larget sum is [4, -1, 2, 1] and the
sum is 6
// Just calculate the sum function

func maxContiguousSum (numbers: [Int]) -> Int? {
    if numbers.count == 1 { // why bother to even run through the
code, quick answer O(1)
        return numbers[0]
    }

    if numbers.count > 1 {
        // trackers to compare
        var currentSum: Int = numbers[0]
        var max = numbers[0] // the secret sauce

        for num in numbers {
            let newSum = currentSum + num

            currentSum = Swift.max(newSum, num)
```

```
            let newMax = Swift.max(max, currentSum) // this number
always grows. Hint: See a trend!?
            max = newMax
        }
        return max
    }
    return nil // returning 0 is just wrong! 0 is a number
}

let test6 = [-2, 1, -3, 4, -1, 2, 1, -5, 4]
let result6 = maxContiguousSum(numbers: test6) // prints a sum of 6
```

Breadth First Search (BFS)

From the **BFS** chapter, there was code to create a **graph** to run **BFS** against. See if your attempt at visualizing the graph matches this (Figure 5).

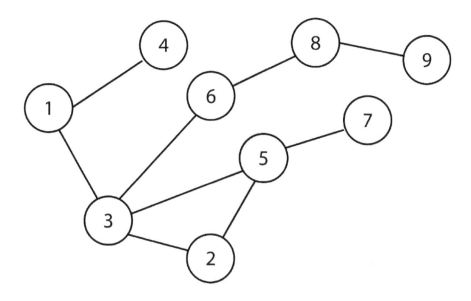

Figure 5. Representation of graph from code example.

Graph diagram from Graph chapter

From the example code in the **Graph** chapter, below is how the **graph** would look like (Figure 6).

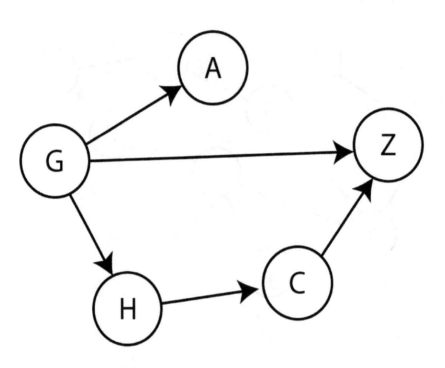

Figure 6. Representation of graph from code example.

References

- https://developer.apple.com/library/ios/documentation/Swift/Conceptual/Swift_Programming_Language/
- https://www.google.com
- https://www.wikipedia.org